ANOTHER
FIELD GUIDE
TO
LITTLE-KNOWN & SELDOM-SEEN
BIRDS
OF NORTH AMERICA

By

Ben L. Sill

Cathryn P. Sill

John C. Sill

Illustrations by
John C. Sill

PEACHTREE PUBLISHERS, LTD.
Atlanta

Published by

PEACHTREE PUBLISHERS, LTD.
494 Armour Circle NE
Atlanta, Georgia 30324

Manufactured in the United States of America

10 9 8 7 6 5 4 3 2 1

Library of Congress Cataloging in Publication Data

Sill, Ben L., 1945-
    Another field guide to little-known & seldom-seen birds of North America / by Ben L. Sill, Cathryn P. Sill, John C. Sill ; illustrations by John C. Sill.
        p.   cm.
    ISBN 0-934601-97-6
    1. Rare birds—North America—Anecdotes. I. Sill, Cathryn P., 1953-   . II. Sill, John. III. Title.
    QL681.S5   1990
    598′.07234′0207—dc20   89-26457
                                                  CIP
Cover design by Laura Ellis

ISBN 0-934601-97-6

To the One who has given us real birds
that bring us so much joy.

CONTENTS

CONTENTS

ACKNOWLEDGMENTS

There are several individuals who helped us a little bit, but not really enough to reveal their names. It is possible that some of the inaccuracies in this volume are due to these persons; however, there is really no need to embarrass Allison, Anna, or even Dr. Rchitxcsmchz. We take full credit for the new and exciting information contained in this volume.

On second thought, we would like to thank Ms. Lois Poteet who was totally in charge of proofreading the manuskrpt.

INTRODUCTION

The ultimate goal of any field guide is to provide accurate information in an easily understood format. With this objective as a beacon, the contents of this volume were developed in a manner to allow even the most inept user to benefit. The guide is divided into three basic sections. First is a guide for novice birders — those still wet under the wings. Next is presented a series of new species. Lastly, a new and innovative approach to bird identification and naming is given.

The first section of the book is aimed at birders who have either recently become interested in birding, or those who, although active for some years, haven't quite gotten the hang of it. Specific information is provided on habitat identification. This section is an outgrowth of years of birding experience by the authors. Since it has become obvious that there are many new species still waiting to be discovered, we have recognized the necessity to help others in this endeavor. A complete step-by-step procedure on how to describe a new species is given. Even someone with only four or five hundred birds on his life list can benefit from the simple method.

The next section is likely the most useful: detailed descriptions and illustrations of 32 new species. Needless to say, no other field guide can provide such up-to-date information. Here again, special attention has been given to utility. While basic information such as range, habitat, and where the birds live is discussed, several innovations are used to help in identification. These include songograms, flight paths, observation hints, identification aids, and specialized equipment. Not only do the full color illustrations include the entire bird, but the accompanying text is usually relevant. There is little doubt that this will be hailed as one of the most complete birding manuals to be published in this century.

The third section gives hints which can make birding a more pleasureable experience. As a bonus, a procedure is presented which allows the user to derive optimum benefit from any new species discovered. In fact we guarantee: you will make more from each new species you find than the cost of this book, or your money will be cheerfully refunded.

GUIDE FOR NOVICE BIRDERS

A. How to Identify Habitat

Field guides constantly refer to the habitat type for particular species. It is imperative that birders be intimately familiar with the specialized terms used for habitat description. The following illustrations are given to assist those who have not been in the field very often.

Habitat Type

Twigs

Water

Ground

Air

B. Identifying New Species

A new species isn't worth much unless you can identify it. Borrowing a technique often used by crime fighters, we suggest that you develop a composite illustration of the bird and use this for final identification. A list of common bird parts is given below to help create the proper description. Even the novice birder will be familiar with most of these parts.

Also shown are several examples of how to and how not to assemble the bird.

BIRD PARTS

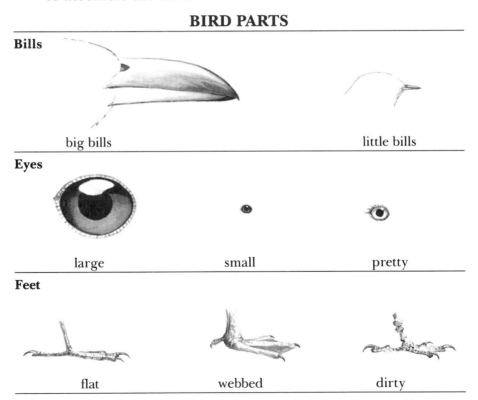

Bills

big bills   little bills

Eyes

large   small   pretty

Feet

flat   webbed   dirty

Necks

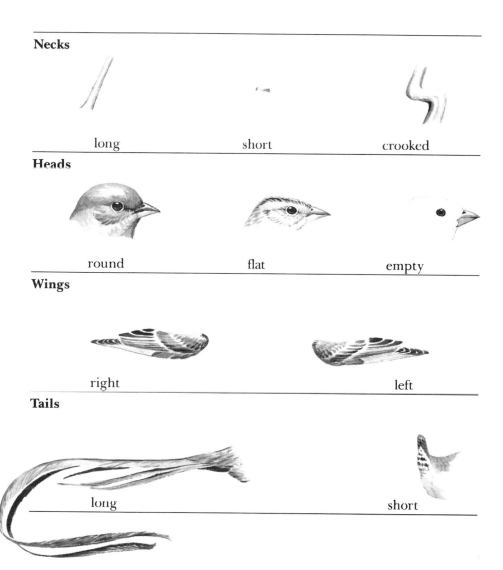

long   short   crooked

Heads

round   flat   empty

Wings

right   left

Tails

long   short

EXAMPLES OF TYPICAL
IDENTIFICATION ASSEMBLIES

Correct Assembly of Parts

Incorrect Assembly of Parts

MORE
LITTLE-KNOWN & SELDOM-SEEN
BIRDS

HIGH DIVING HERON
Kamakaze icthygrabbus

Although this bird is considered a heron, its classification at this point is questionable. It is distinguished from diving birds of the same size by its long legs, from birds of prey by its long bill, and from short-necked birds by its long neck. The High Diving Heron feeds almost exclusively on catfish and other bottom dwelling species with total disregard for its own safety. Depending on water clarity, depth of prey, and degree of difficulty, diving scores can range from 7.5 to 9.

BRUSH   HERON

2

HIGH DIVING HERON

MANGROVE PENGUIN
Tuxedo verdantus

This northernmost of the penguins has acclimated to the mangrove swamps of tropical North America to avoid predation by Killer Whales. Although sunburn has caused some setbacks, the population has been slowly increasing and several stable colonies have been located in Florida. However, some environmentalists are concerned about the proximity of local aquariums and marine shows. They fear that structural failures may result in the mass escape of Killer Whales, thus decimating the Mangrove Penguin population.

OBSERVATION HINT Occasionally a homesick bird will be seen in iceberg lettuce fields.

MANGROVE PENGUIN

DOWRY DUCK
Anas seductorii

The drab female of this species spends much of her time stocking a hope nest in order to attract a mate. Recent studies indicate that the drake is most readily enticed by shotgun shells. Spent shells are most often collected, but live shells sometimes find their way into the nest. Occasionally on very hot days, explosive incubation episodes may occur. The Dowry Duck's mating habits give new meaning to the term shotgun wedding.

OBSERVATION HINT   It is relatively easy to locate where nests used to be. Just look for small craters.

DOWRY DUCK

SPLIT RAIL

Alticrotch thighlongus

One seldom encounters this uncommon bird since there aren't very many of them. The Split Rail has the ability to walk through tall marsh grass early in the morning without getting any dew on his belly although it is not obvious how this is an advantage. Split Rails have some difficulty in squatting and thus build rather tall nests. Extensive sub-nest video observations indicate that egg laying in this species can be a long drawn out process.

SPLIT RAIL

URBAN SNIPE

Urbanus migratorius

The ancestors of the Urban Snipe lived in open fields and green meadows. Present day members of this species have modified their behavior to spend a portion of the day in an urban setting. Flocks fly into the city each morning where they make their living in the gutters and return to the open country in the afternoon. This activity is termed commuter migration. In recent years it has been noticed that this species seems to be attracted to television. Flocks sometimes delay their homeward flight and gather outside appliance stores to watch the early evening game shows. Its song — an insistent "honk, honk" — is heard most often from birds in the rear of the flock.

OBSERVATION HINT Often seen preening at traffic lights.

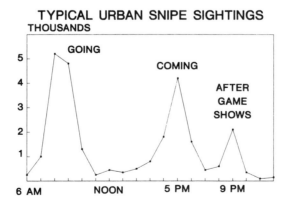

URBAN SNIPE

DREDGER

Diggus r. strainerii

This largest of shorebirds has evolved a whale-like baleen in the front of its bill, enabling it to effectively filter small subterranean arthroscopes from sandy beaches. Prized for this baleen, it was hunted ruthlessly by whaling vessels. However, most ships went aground before harpooning the unwary birds on the beach. Even though the Dredger resembles other shorebirds in coloration, with practice it can usually be picked out of a mixed flock.

IDENTIFICATION AID   Call.

TYPICAL SHOREBIRD:

peep

DREDGER:

PEEP!

DREDGER

DUFFER SHANK

Birdie impossibilus

The Duffer Shank is locally common in its highly specialized habitat consisting of fairly large grassy areas with occasional wooded borders. The egg is a small white sphere with green flecks and a dimpled appearance. For nest sites, Shanks seem to choose the edges of small isolated sandy areas. Nesting instincts for this species are very strong and they will often brood any small round white object they find. Where man's activities overlap, this behavioral trait has caused some problems. The Duffer Shank is one of the few birds that apparently has no instinctive song, but rather one learned from its environment. While there is some variation, the song generally goes -

"#?!@@!!#X&@&&$#"

followed by a loud, "BLAST IT!!"

OBSERVATION HINT Can occasionally be found on driving ranges. However, mortality rates are quite high.

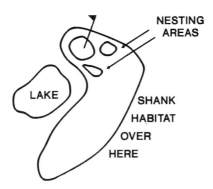

14

DUFFER SHANK

LESSER NESSIE

Pseudomonstersaurus obscurus

Found primarily on fog enshrouded lakes in northern Canada, the Lesser Nessie has been the object of much confusion regarding its classification. It has variously been considered an otter, a sea slug, Ogopogo, and a ripple on the water. Actually we now know that it is a new species of wading bird. Although we have only a single photograph taken under foggy conditions, the description has been completed from several reliable eyewitness accounts. However, these individuals report that the portion of the bird which shows above the surface is generally out of focus.

OBSERVATION HINT   It helps to have a vivid imagination.

LESSER NESSIE

35 mm SLR, 100-500 zoom, F5.6, ASA 25, Color Film, Shutter speed 1/125, Prefocussed.

ROLLING ATROCIOUS CARRION EATER (RACE)

Tumblus ingestus mortis on the via

The RACE is the only known flightless vulture. This bird's protective coloration causes it to appear remarkably like a puff of diesel exhaust. Since the RACE nests in culverts, there is frequent nest destruction during wet weather. Due to the valuable service this bird performs on our highways, ODOR* is prominent in trying to protect this species by initiating a captive breeding program. In addition, to ensure a consistently high standard of food procurement for the RACE, STENCH** was formed. Although applicants are few, this subdiscipline of ornithology is ripe with opportunity.

OBSERVATION HINT Look for RACE tracks.

SPECIALIZED EQUIPMENT Road maps supplied by ROT***.

*Office of Development of Overland Roadways
**Society To Evaluate Novice Carrion Handlers
***Regional Office of Transportation

ROLLING ATROCIOUS CARRION EATER (RACE)

DINING

FIXED-WING FALCON
Falco rigidis

Superficially, this medium sized falcon appears to be a Peregrine, but unless the bird is viewed while perched, positive identification is difficult. Through the eons, the wings of this bird have become fused into an outstretched position. As a result, the Fixed-Wing Falcon does not flap and its flight is like that of a toy airplane. It has a great deal of difficulty perching in a stiff breeze. When air currents are insufficient to allow soaring, this bird has been known to rapidly move its tail up and down to provide forward speed, although this rhythmic motion causes some individuals to become airsick.

OBSERVATION HINT   Nesting sites can be most easily located when the female is laying the eggs since she periodically utters a call of O-o-o-o-o-o-o-w!!!!!

FIXED-WING FALCON

EGG

POWERED FLIGHT

YELLOW-BELLIED PRAIRIE CHICKEN
Multiphobius multiphobius

This uncommon bird of the prairie is scarce and local, having fled from much of its former range. It always backs away from confrontations, and has been known to retreat from aggressive snails. The Yellow-Bellied Prairie Chicken is even afraid of members of its own species, which results in poor nesting success. Other phobias which afflict this bird are:

Grainophobia:	fear of its primary food
Flatophobia:	fear of open spaces
Fixedophobia:	fear of standing still
Pediaphobia:	fear of walking
Sprintophobia:	fear of running
Aerophobia:	fear of flying
Phobiaphobia:	fear of fear

It is a mystery how natural selection could have overlooked such an obvious candidate for extinction.

SPECIALIZED TRAINING   A degree in ornipsychology.

Yellow-Bellied Prairie Chicken

Nearsighted Bat Owl

Invertus myopius

This recently discovered owl of abandoned farm buildings has many behavioral traits which set it apart from more common owls. It roosts during the day by hanging upside down and unlike other owls, it sees quite poorly. After dusk, the Bat Owl begins feeding, primarily on small rodents. It often mistakes its intended prey, and has been known to attack corn cobs and cow patties. Nests are securely attached to rafters and other building supports. Incubation successes are generally low since every time the owl leaves the nest, the eggs fall out.

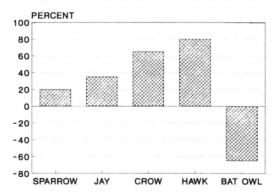

NESTING SUCCESS OF VARIOUS BIRDS

24

NEARSIGHTED BAT OWL

WILL

Hypotheticus willus

Dedicated ornithologists have spent much of the last decade researching the possible existence of the Will. The results of this study indicate that the size and song of the birds in this family have a direct relationship to the number of letters in their name. To demonstrate the scientific method used, this information is plotted below. It stands to reason that the Will, with 4 letters in his name, has a length of about 5 inches and a single note song. The name Willard has been proposed by the Institute for Naming Birds; however, this two syllable name will be accepted only if the species can be taught a new song and can be made to grow longer.

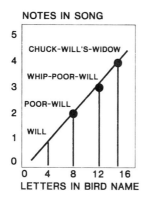

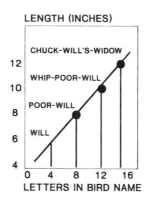

WILLS

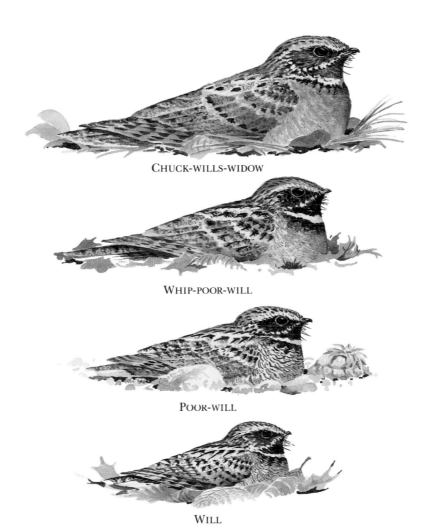

CHUCK-WILLS-WIDOW

WHIP-POOR-WILL

POOR-WILL

WILL

GREY-GREEN LICHEN MIMIC
Petriflorus imitatus

Most people are not very excited about lichen. The same is true in the animal world (except for a caribou now and then). As a result, hungry animals have little desire to eat a lichen or anything that looks like a lichen. It is this fact that has made the Lichen Mimic so successful. The Lichen Mimic chick resembles other young birds, but as it matures, the bird gets flatter and flatter and both eyes migrate to the top of its head. This movement is known as intracranial optic migration. With this modification, their camouflage is so good that we just don't know how many of these birds there really are. Song is a flat note.

OBSERVATION HINT   Look for two eyes staring at you from lichen covered rocks.

SPECIALIZED EQUIPMENT   Unabridged Field Guide to the Lichens of North America

GREY-GREEN LICHEN MIMIC

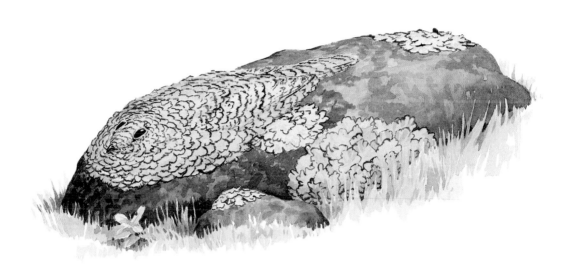

EGG

CROSSCUT SAWBILL
Dendrochoppus forestii

This denizen of the deep woods is never found far from trees. The beak of the Sawbill is uniquely adapted for cutting; it saws nesting material from the higher limbs and uses regurgitated sawdust as food for the young. The Sawbill also saws open various nuts for food while holding them in its claws. Due to feeding accidents, most mature Sawbills have very short toes. To date the Sawbill has not been required to obtain Forest Service permits; however, rumors indicate that this is under consideration in Washington. Note that the Circular Sawbill is believed extinct.

OBSERVATION HINT   Flocks of Sawbills often clear cut large areas.

Yellow Jasmine Shrike
Floraimpalus dixieii

Found throughout the Deep South, the Yellow Jasmine Shrike is the daintiest of the North American Shrikes. In contrast to others in its family, Jasmine Shrikes are highly social, often gathering in small but animated groups. It is a thrilling experience to see a flock of these lovely birds flitting around cascading garlands of golden jasmine blossoms. Each bird makes its debut in the spring clad in exquisite plumage of vibrant yellow highlighted by jet black wings with matching beak and feet. The wings and tail are accented with lacy white edgings. Its call is a soft drawn out "ya'll".

OBSERVATION HINT   This small, delicate butcherbird can be easily found in the spring by looking for jasmine blooms impaled on barbed wire fences or thorn bushes. Do not confuse with the Yellow Jasmine Shrike Imitator which impales plastic flowers.

YELLOW JASMINE SHRIKE

CRIMSON PUFFLET

Sphericus inflatus

Little was known about this bright red bird until a recent study sponsored by Pufflets International showed it to be a unique species. The Pufflet demonstrates a behavior biologists refer to as unbalanced halation. It inhales more than it exhales. This defense mechanism is apparently what has saved the Crimson Pufflet from extinction: it inhales when threatened and while bloated is difficult to eat. Puffed Pufflets have a highly erratic defense flight. Song is a long wheeze.

OBSERVATION HINT An effective decoy can be made by using a large red apple and attaching a cherry for the head.

P.S. Recipes for decoy pie are available from Pufflets International.

CRIMSON PUFFLET

DEFENSE POSTURE   DEFENSE FLIGHT

BLUE DART

Azure missilii

This fast flying predator of clear skies and open spaces is almost perfectly camouflaged. Blue Darts feed on flying insects, most often attacking them out of the blue. While juvenile birds will occasionally go after bugs crawling on tree trunks, this behavior is seldom repeated. Darts have been known to suffer severe beak damage when feeding during hail storms. It is difficult to locate the bird by its call since the sound arrives after the bird is long gone.

SPECIALIZED EQUIPMENT   Fly rod with an assortment of dry flies. Please use barbless hooks.

FLIGHT PATHS

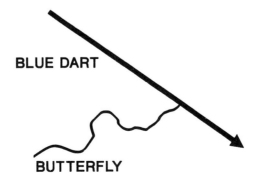

BLUE DART

BUTTERFLY

BLUE DART

FEEDING

JUVENILE

NORTHERN CHZIRTMAQUEYST IXCTYLMABKINRLET

Multitudinous consonantii

This small bird of the northern forests hasn't been studied since no one knows how to pronounce its name. According to Dr. Cstzwyabntl Rchitxcsmchz (who found and named this bird), they rymcdksching, wvcopeedle, and occasionally exaksylch. The consensus in the birding community is that the most desirable action is for Dr. Rchitxcsmchz to rename it something like Common Squeaker. Once this is done, any number of highly qualified scientists would be willing to study the bird and write up their findings for the layman. The facing illustration is the artist's conception of the Ixctylmabkinrlet based on data provided via personal communication with Dr. Rchitxcsmchz. In fact, we must thank him for being one of the first individuals to use our composite parts method for bird identification (see the front section of this Guide).

OBSERVATION HINT   This bird sings consonantly.

Northern Chzirtmaqueyst
Ixctylmabkinrlet

XQQ

SCREAMER TIT

Magnus decibelii

The Screamer Tit is the only bird known to use its call both as a defense mechanism and for securing its food. Researchers tell of hawks with shattered beaks, and many pairs of binoculars have been damaged by being within earshot of this species. Since Screamer Tits form large flocks, most adult birds are stone deaf. The Screamer Tit uses vocaloblastosis to stun caterpillars which are then devoured. To protect the eggs from breaking, this bird does not sing during the incubation period. Nests are best located by listening for the song of the embryo. At the time of hatching, the embryo increases its volume.

OBSERVATION HINT Caution! Misguided birders sometimes show up at rock concerts thinking they have discovered a flock of Screamer Tits.

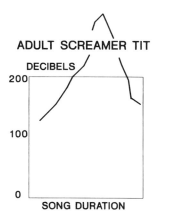

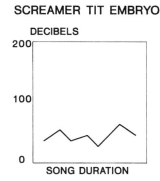

SCREAMER TIT

HATCHING

Double-Crested Impulse Layer

Albuminus ejectus

This little bird of mature forests is fidgety and constantly in motion. For years it was thought that low reproductive rates occurred because of faulty nest construction. However, recent studies indicate clearly that this is not the case. The highly sensitive female of this species reacts to environmental stresses by laying her eggs rapidly and anywhere. Scientists have begun to refer to this behavior as the egg drop syndrome. Caution: avoid making loud noises when walking beneath tall trees.

OBSERVATION HINT   Listen for soft splat, splat sounds. If this doesn't work, examine the branches for hanging yolks.

SPECIALIZED EQUIPMENT   Slicker with a hood.

DOUBLE-CRESTED IMPULSE LAYER

EGG

REAR-TAILED EVADER

Mostus absentus

Although elusive, this is one of the most commonly seen birds in North America. Anyone who is serious about birding will have encountered this species, even if a positive identification was not possible. Often called an "Itjustflew" by birders, it is best identified quickly and without requiring too much burdensome information such as field marks. Quite often, more is known about the tree it was perched in than about the bird itself. Song is a fading series of notes, seldom heard in its entirety.

OBSERVATION HINT   When you think you have seen an Evader, be confident, and sing out to your birding companions: "I just saw a Rear-Tailed Evader." DO NOT ALLOW ANY DOUBT TO CREEP INTO YOUR VOICE.

SPECIALIZED EQUIPMENT   A bird field guide is not needed.

IDENTIFICATION AID   One way to positively identify the Rear-tailed Evader is by a feather count as shown in the figure below.

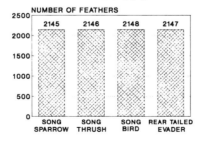

FEATHER COUNT

REAR-TAILED EVADER

GREATER WANDERING VAGRANT

formerly Casualus wanderii

now Marsupialus wanderii

Upon arrival in the spring, this species wanders in a seemingly erratic pattern over much of North America before returning somewhere south in the fall. A detailed description of this bird was given in the first volume of this field guide. At that time it was believed that the Vagrant carried its nest with it on its travels. With some embarrassment, we must admit that we may have been incorrect. What we now think is that the Vagrant carries its young in a belly pouch. While we are more confident than ever, what we really need to remove all doubts is a captured specimen. Since dead birds do not mail well, please send photographs only to:

Vagrant Research Project
16 Boardwalk Ave.
Ocean View, KS

GREATER WANDERING VAGRANT

FORMER THEORY

CURRENT THEORY

Narrow-Waisted Cinch

Corsettus tightus

This fetching relative of the finch has been popular with other birds for years, only recently coming to the attention of people. One of the few examples in the bird kingdom of the female being more attractive than the male, this beautiful bird often attracts males of many different species with its generic courtship display. In addition to its elegant plumage, its claws are painted with berry juice. All in all, this bird is quite a looker. Although it doesn't call, its presence can be determined from the calls of the attending males, a loud "wheet wheeo".

OBSERVATION HINT   Generally found in the midst of a flock of discerning males.

NARROW-WAISTED CINCH

GREATER NOXIOUS GROSSBIRD
Incredibilus disgustus

While examples of this new species have been observed for years, to date ornithologists have not had the stomach to fully describe its behavior. Both sexes exhibit a wide variety of disgusting habits, including belching, leaving a ring around their dust bath, and scratching their wing pits in public. The males and females dislike each other, and occupy separate ranges. The few young that are raised quickly acquire obnoxious habits, and many young birds fall from their perch while trying to outgross each other. Breeding success is greatest where the male and female ranges overlap. Its song is terrible.

OBSERVATION HINT   Best located from downwind.

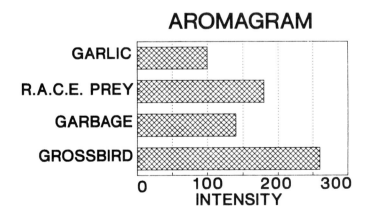

50

GREATER NOXIOUS GROSSBIRD

PREENING

BROWED MEGABRAIN

Avianus intellectus

This really smart bird is able to match wits with most birders. Its breeding plumage has even been likened to graduation regalia. Megabrains spend much of their time with small scale creative endeavors and in developing elaborate ways to avoid detection. Some researchers believe that there are two subspecies of the Megabrain, told apart by the amount of philosophizing they do. These subspecies have been named the Highbrow Megabrain and the Lowbrow Megabrain. Although the two birds look very much alike, they are best differentiated by their outlook on life. The Highbrow lives by "I think, therefore I am" while the Lowbrow uses "I instinct, therefore it happens."

OBSERVATION HINT   The two subspecies can be told apart by how long it takes the bird to give up on getting seeds taped to the inside of your window: Highbrow Megabrain — 10 to 15 seconds; Lowbrow Megabrain — several days or until it weakens from hunger.

Browed Megabrain

Lowbrow

Highbrow

RESPLENDENT BAYOU SWINGER

Tarzanus similaris

(Formerly the Long-Nosed Macaw)

This bird has migrated from South America in recent years and now is found in many of the remote swamps along the Gulf Coast. The Swinger's beak has evolved, allowing it to hang from small branches rather than perching like more typical birds. It has lost its ability to fly and maneuvers in the forest by swinging from branch to branch. The song of the Resplendent Bayou Swinger is "aahh-ee-ah-ee-ah-ahh-ee-ah-ee-ah-ahhh", repeated several times for effect. Don't be confused by the "a-a-a-a-a-a-a-a-oh-no" sound it makes when it misses a limb.

FLIGHT PATH

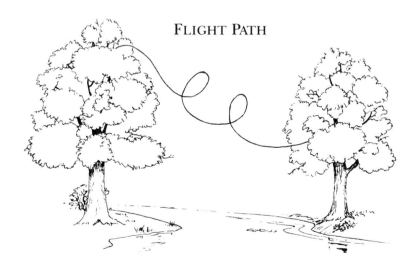

Resplendent Bayou Swinger

PIED PIPER

Hamlin tooterii

The long bill and undulating flight of this songbird is quite distinctive. The pied, black and white plumage is an excellent field mark, but the Piper is best known for his song. Though their songs vary widely, Pipers have a common prefix which serves as a warmup. With a three octave range, the Piper can reproduce most classical scores and by restricting his volume to loud, he can handle most contemporary music. This delightful visitor to yard and garden is a welcome and cheery addition to any backyard bird population. It is important to note however, that the Pied Piper tends to attract rats and small children.

SONGOGRAM   Only warmup song is shown.

PIED PIPER

GREEN SUBUPPERLET
Variagatus subsuperioranus

The Green Subupperlet is found primarily in the dense underbrush of Southern evergreen shrub bogs where it feeds on slimy things. An attractive subspecies of this bird, the Red Winged Green Subupperlet inhabits a narow band just to the north of the Green Subupperlet. Moving further north we find in succession, a subsubspecies, the Partly Red Green Subupperlet, and the subsubsubspecies, the Mostly Red Green Subupperlet. Finally on the northernmost part of its range, we find the Red Green Subupperlet subsubsubsubspecies. Occasionally one of these northern birds will revert to the all green southern form and is called simply the Green Red Green Subupperlet.

GREEN SUBUPPERLET

GREEN SUBUPPERLET

RED WINGED GREEN SUBUPPERLET

PARTLY RED GREEN SUBUPPERLET

MOSTLY RED GREEN SUBUPPERLET

RED GREEN SUBUPPERLET

GREEN RED GREEN SUBUPPERLET

BROAD-BILLED BABBLER

Miscellaneous verbosus

This striking bird can sometimes be located while babbling from an exposed perch, however since it generally makes noise most of the time one can usually find it by just being quiet for a while and listening to the constant effusion of bird-type noises which can come from bushes or low trees so long as the Babbler hasn't migrated or has a sore throat which doesn't occur very often since his metabolism is geared up for an endless stream of bird words that apparently are useful in helping the Babblers to locate each other even in dense underbrush or thick fogs and also probably to help the young to stay with the family group after they are hatched in early summer from brightly colored eggs laid in a delicately woven nest of moss and other soft things which are used to keep the eggs from breaking while they are being sat on.

OBSERVATION HINT Call is a whistled "cheer up, cheer up, drink your tea, old Sam Peabody, Oh Canada, cheery cheerio, witchety witchety, pee o wee, chickadee dee dee, Bob White, what cheer, who cooks for you all, quick three beers," repeated several times a second.

BROAD-BILLED BABBLER

SILHOUETTE WARBLER

Dendroica unidimensionalis

The identity of this species has been pieced together using numerous reports from across the continent. It seems that this bird is most often active near dusk, or on cloudy days high in trees. While there are no obvious field marks, this in itself serves as a basis for identification. It is the only warbler-sized bird without field marks such as wing bars, breast markings and a colored cap. It does have black outer tail feathers and a black eye ring. The overall coloring of the bird is flat black.

SILHOUETTE WARBLER

♂

♀

FRONT VIEW

REAR VIEW

EGG

NEEDLE-TAILED WARBLER
Posterius pointus

After considerable study, we have classified this oddly shaped bird as a warbler even though it seems more sparrow-like. Its wings are made from transparent feathers and the number of feathers per wing is reduced to two. Rather than having the nice rounded belly of most warblers, it is quite skinny. It does eat insects, but doesn't sing very loudly. Its legs are very short with only the toes showing. Despite these differences, we are proud to introduce here, for the first time, the Needle-tailed Warbler.

OBSERVATION HINT   Often perches on the tips of fishing poles.

NOTE TO NOVICE BIRDERS   Early indications are that Posterius is a potentially large genus with the Needle-tailed Warbler being only the first species in this genus to be discovered and named. Therefore, if you want to get out there and discover a new species, this may be your best chance.

Needle-tailed Warbler

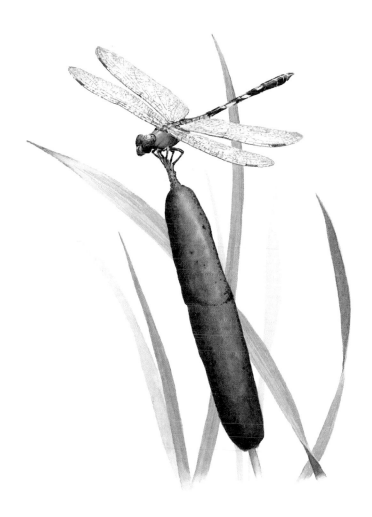

HINTS TO MAKE YOUR BIRDING LIFE
MORE PRODUCTIVE

A. What to Say When Birding in a Group

These are hints which can help prevent embarrassing situations for the novice birder.

At the Seashore

Don't Say: Golly days, all those little birds look just alike!

Do Say: We need better light to identify those peeps.

In the Forest

Don't Say: I can't see anything for these stupid trees.

Do Say: Isn't it exhilarating trying to see those tiny warblers among all the leaves?

From the Car

Don't Say: Boy this sure is an easy way to list a bunch of birds.

Do Say: A car certainly makes a good blind.

In a Boat

Don't Say: These waves sure make it hard to keep lunch down.
Do Say: These waves sure make it hard to focus on the birds.

In a Backyard

Don't Say: When birds bash themselves into your picture window, do you feed them to your cat?
Do Say: What kind of thistle seed do you buy?

In a Blind

Don't Say: Do you mind if I play the radio?
Do Say: Have you seen anything good?

B. How to Take Full Credit
for New Species You Discover

Surprisingly, little information is available regarding the steps necessary to ensure that any new species which you discover is rightly credited to you. We feel it is important that birders be given ample opportunity to capitalize on the fame which comes with identification of a new species. To this end, we suggest a plan of action to help exploit your new species to the fullest. Many of these items are secrets which we have personally used for years, and we now feel it is appropriate to share these with the rest of the birding world. So if you are serious about finding new species, try the suggestions given below:

1. BIRD ALONE — Even your best birding friend may try to scoop you on a species which you rightly discovered.

2. SKETCH THE BIRD — Photos can be retouched and are therefore considered unreliable.

3. NAME THE BIRD — Don't worry about any silly protocol, just go ahead and name the bird. Make sure it is a name that is replete with adjectives. If you have trouble coming up with ideas for a meaningful bird name, you might try the suggestions outlined here.

From the table below
pick any one word from each column

Common	light-headed	orange	bird
Greater	blue-kneed	feathered	bird
Fast	gravel-voiced	pretty	bird
Elusive	heavy-set	basic	bird
Inferior	semi-tropical	migratory	bird
Superior	mauve-tailed	sedentary	bird
Drowsy	brownish-red	gargantuan	bird
Anxious	reddish-brown	flappy	bird
Clumsy	acting	treetop	birdlet

You can always name the bird after yourself (unless you use a pseudonym). This is easily done by substituting your name for the word in the first column above. This approach is the only foolproof method of ensuring that your name will be remembered in the annals of science.

Example:

Harry's gravel-voiced flappy bird

4. USE THE NAME: It is important to use the name of your new bird as though it has been around for years. Use it in letters and casual conversation . Once it is in common usage, it will become a part of our heritage.

5. LOOK FOR EXPOSURE: Try to interest talk show hosts in interviewing you (get an agent if necessary). These shows are usually on the lookout for marginal individuals.

While we can't be sure that the approach given above will always work, we have been using it for years and no one is the wiser.

FIELD NOTES

FIELD NOTES

FIELD NOTES

FIELD NOTES

ABOUT THE AUTHORS

JOHN SILL, a native of North Carolina, holds a B.S. in wildlife biology from North Carolina State University. Combining his knowledge of wildlife and his artistic skill, he has gained a reputation as a wildlife artist and received prizes throughout the Southeast. Sill has provided illustrations for Audubon bird identification calendars and is also the illustrator of *Field Guide to the Birds Coloring Book* (Houghton Mifflin, 1982), *The Guide to Bird Behavior,* vol. II in Little Brown's *Stokes Nature Guide* series and *A Field Guide to Little-Known & Seldom-Seen Birds of North America* (Peachtree, 1988) which he coauthored with Cathryn and Ben Sill.

CATHRYN SILL teaches at an elementary school in Franklin, North Carolina, and, like her husband John, enjoys birding and nature photography in her leisure time. She is presently writing a children's book about birds.

BEN SILL, John's brother, lives with his wife and two daughters in Clemson, South Carolina, where he is a Professor of Civil Engineering at Clemson University. Ben is also an avid birder.